Finn Goes to the Toilet

Finn Goes to the Toilet

Written and Illustrated by Teresa Amy Lewis
Contributions by Finley Bishop Lewis

Copyright © 2023 by Teresa Amy Lewis

All rights reserved.

No part of this publication may be reproduced, distributed, or transmitted in any form or by any means, including photocopying, recording, or other electronic or mechanical methods, without the prior written permission of the publisher, except as permitted by U.S. copyright law. For permission requests, contact TALewisDesign@gmail.com.

Text in this book is set in My Handwriting, a custom creation.
Book Cover and Illustrations by Teresa Amy Lewis
First Edition April 2023

To my partner in everything, you are my best friend and my refuge. Thank you for helping create this amazing family and for helping to keep it all together. I can't wait to see what's next!

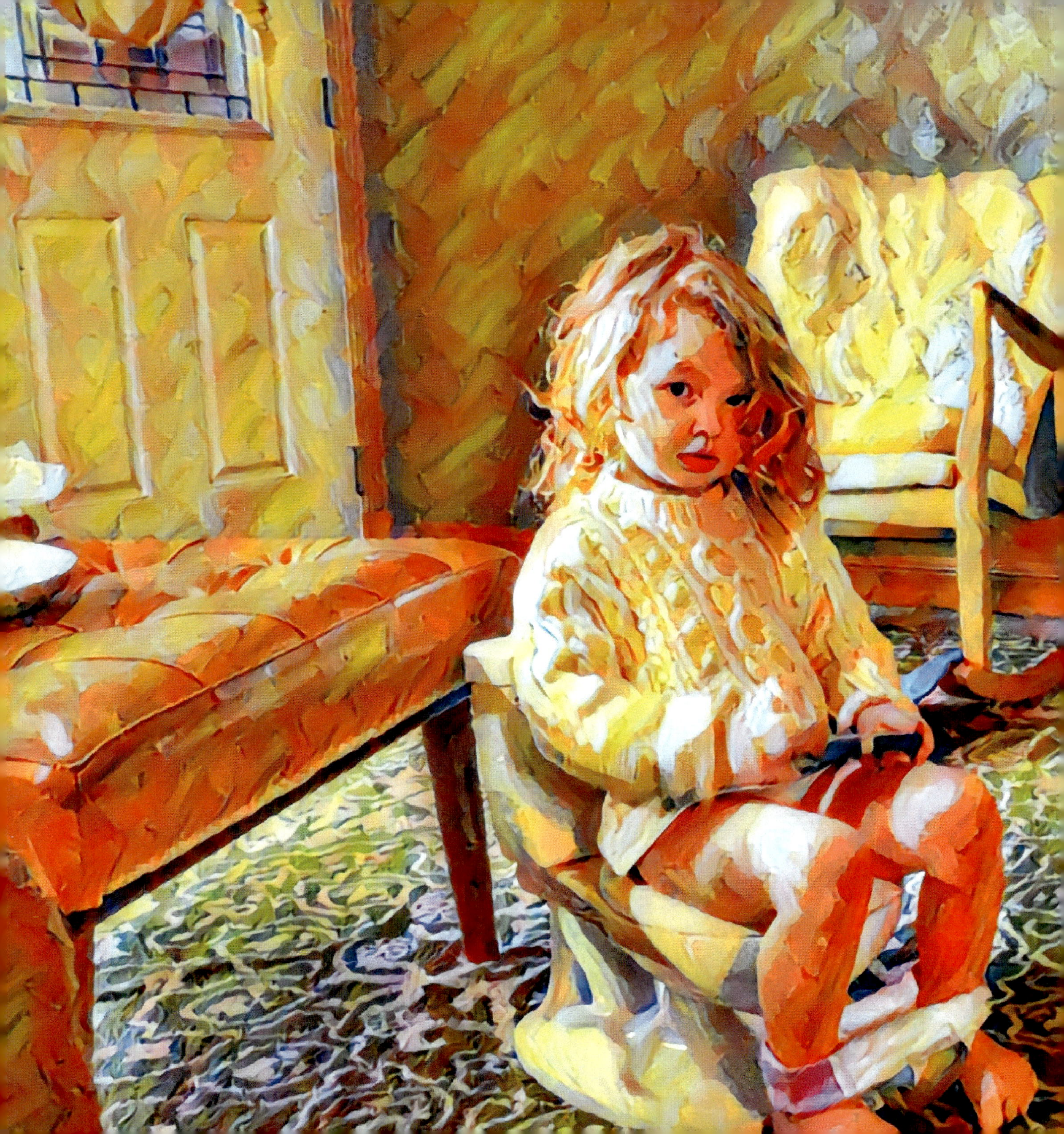

My name is Finley and I want to grow up to be independent. Independent means I can do things by myself. Using the toilet is something I can do on my own!

I am proud to be able to use the toilet all by myself!

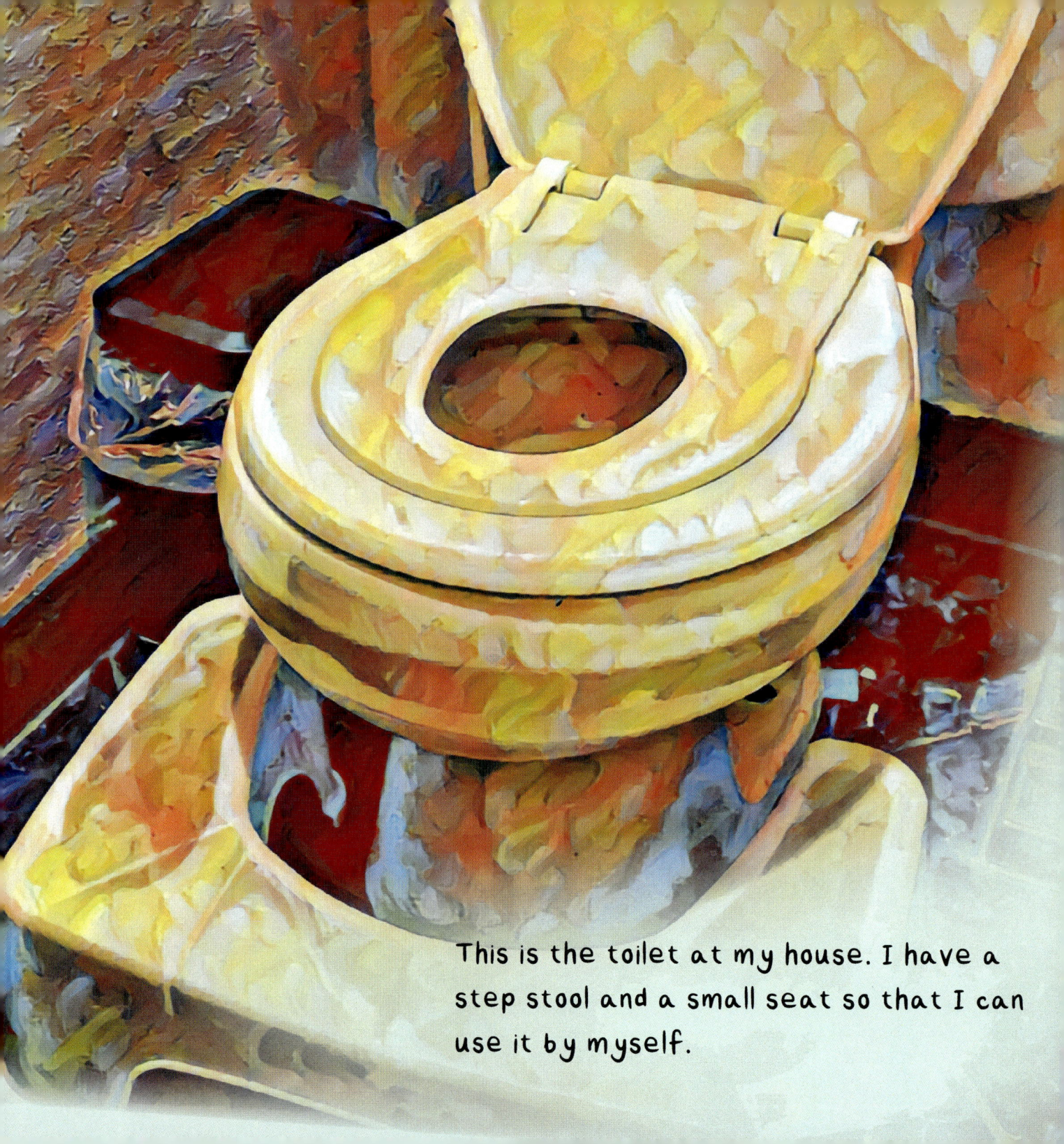

This is the toilet at my house. I have a step stool and a small seat so that I can use it by myself.

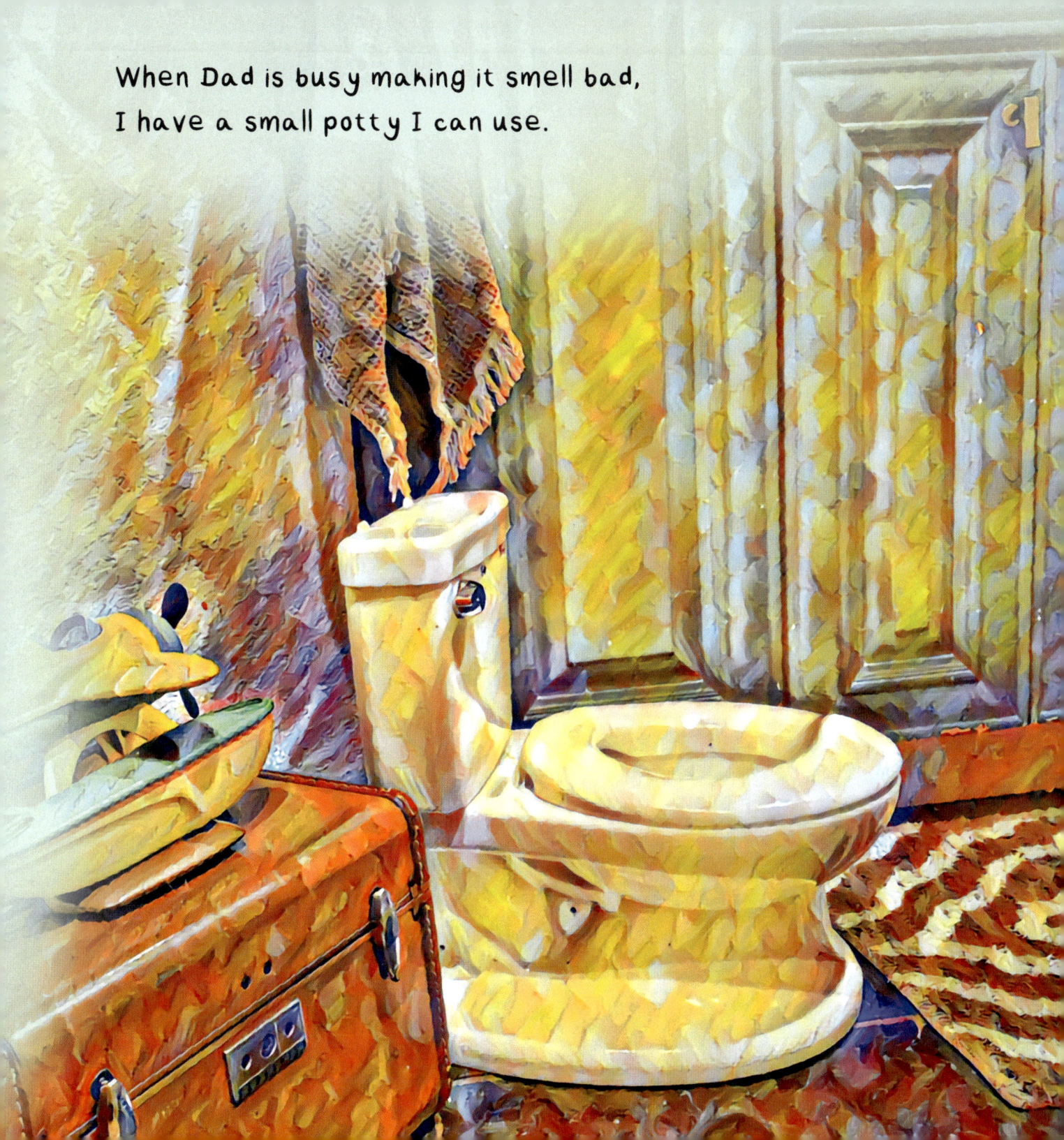

When Dad is busy making it smell bad,
I have a small potty I can use.

There are specific feelings I get when I have to pee or poop. I feel it in my tummy, below my belly button or in my butt. Sometimes I start to wiggle and squirm.

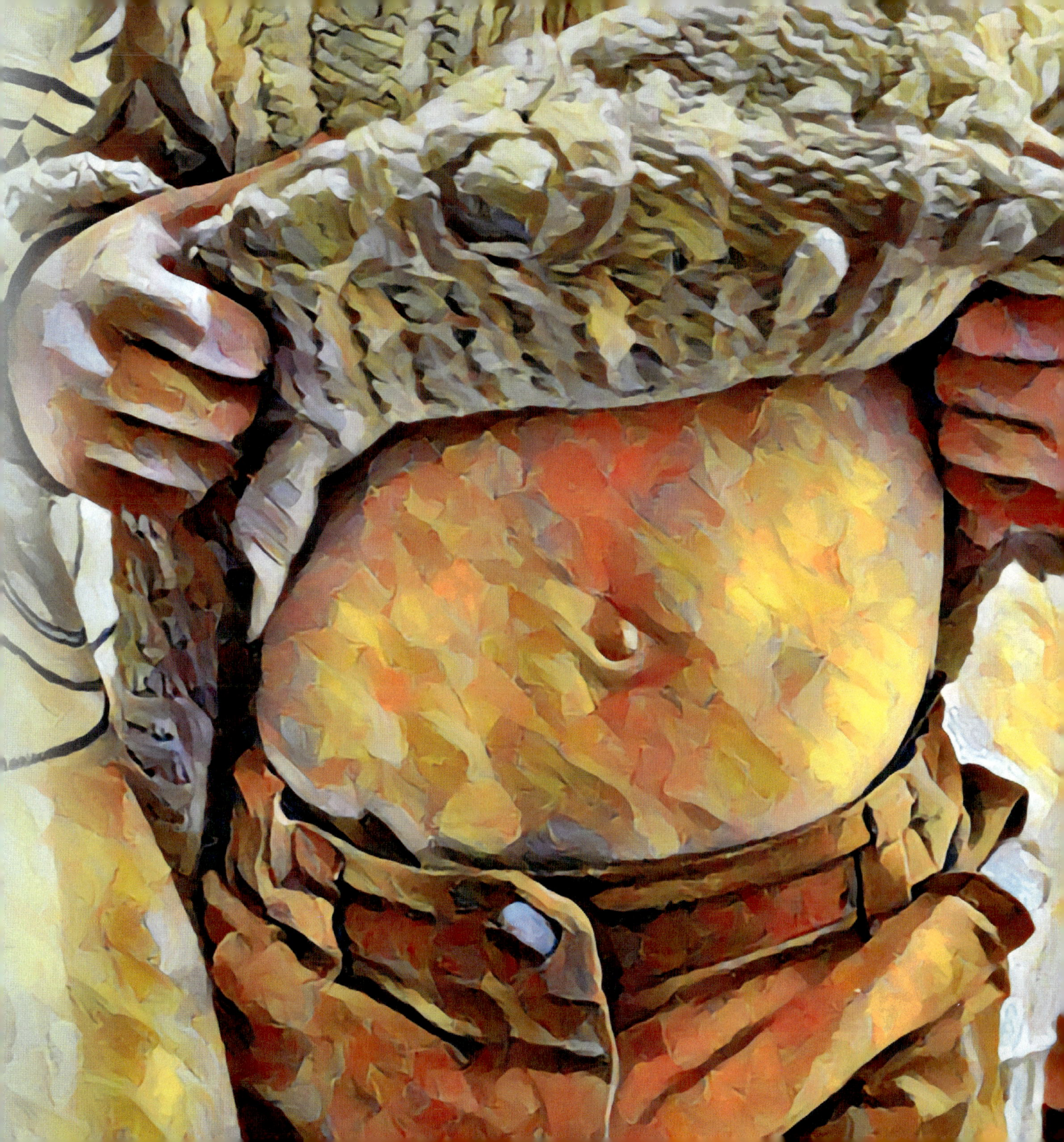

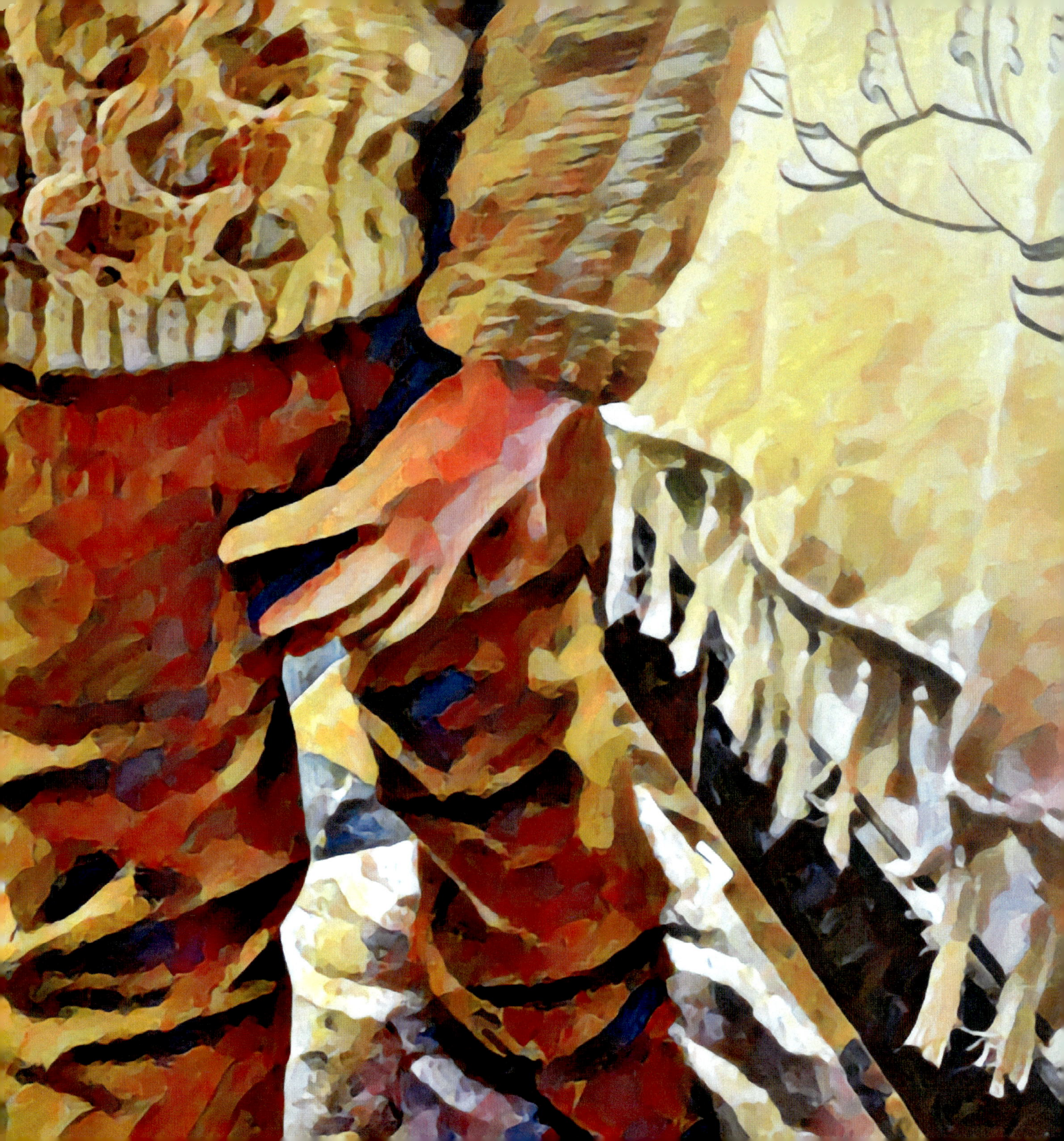

What does it feel like when you have to go pee?

What about when you have to go poop?

I might be playing outside or watching my tablet. When I get the feeling, I know to rush to the bathroom right away.

If I need help, I can ask, but I always try to figure it out by myself.

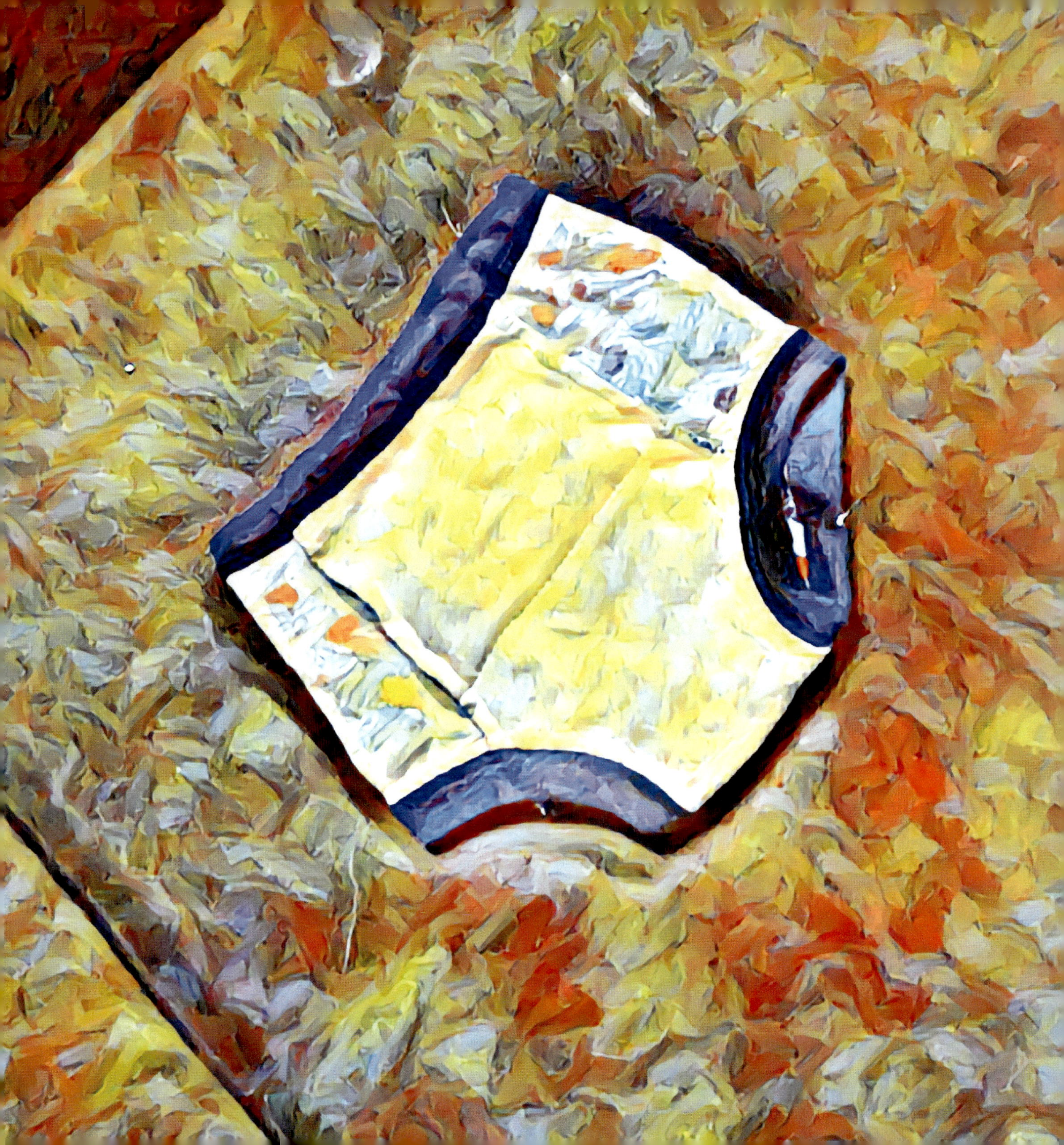

If I wait too long I might have an accident. An accident is when I pee or poop in my underwear.

I hate it! YUCK!

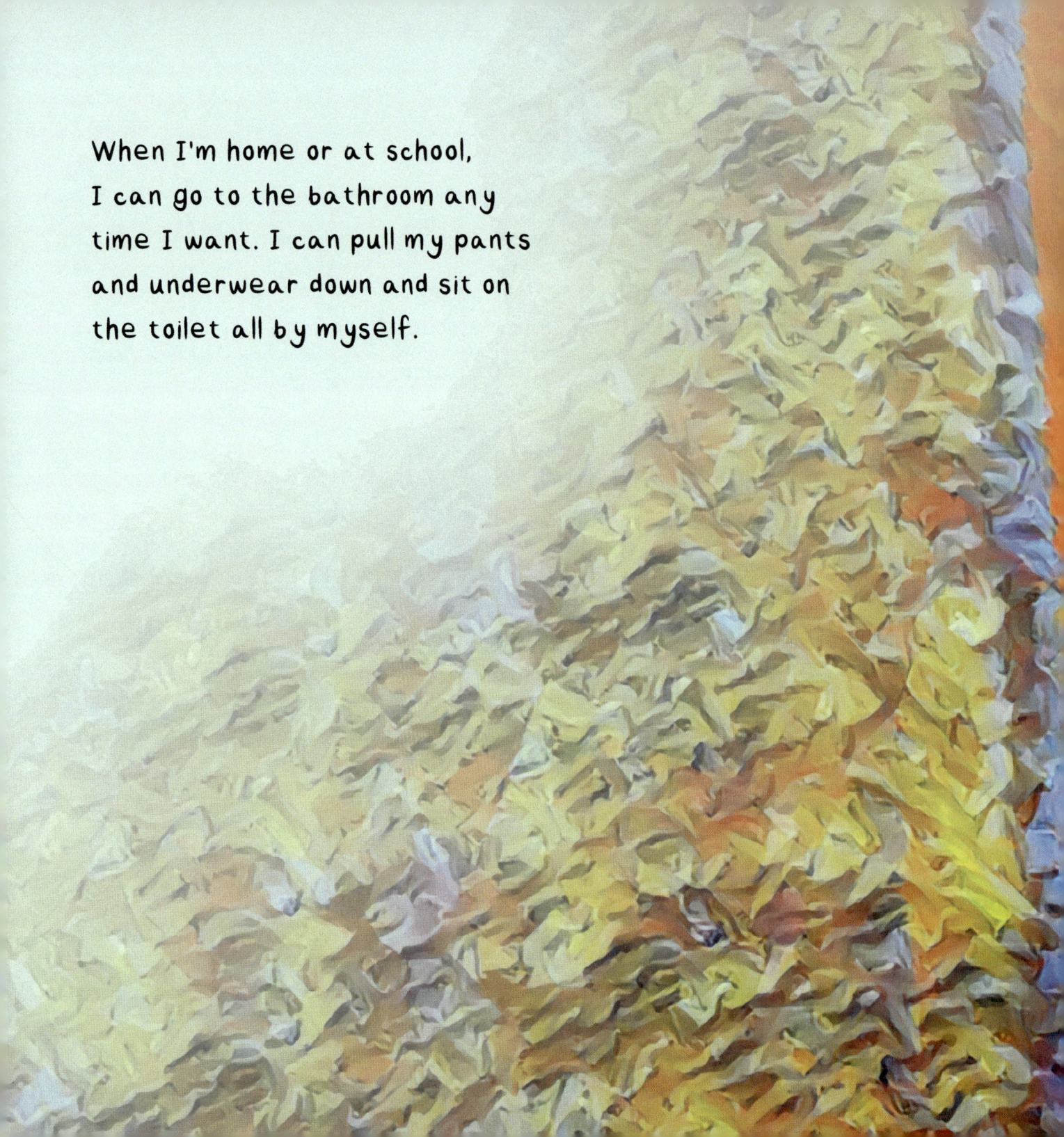

When I'm home or at school, I can go to the bathroom any time I want. I can pull my pants and underwear down and sit on the toilet all by myself.

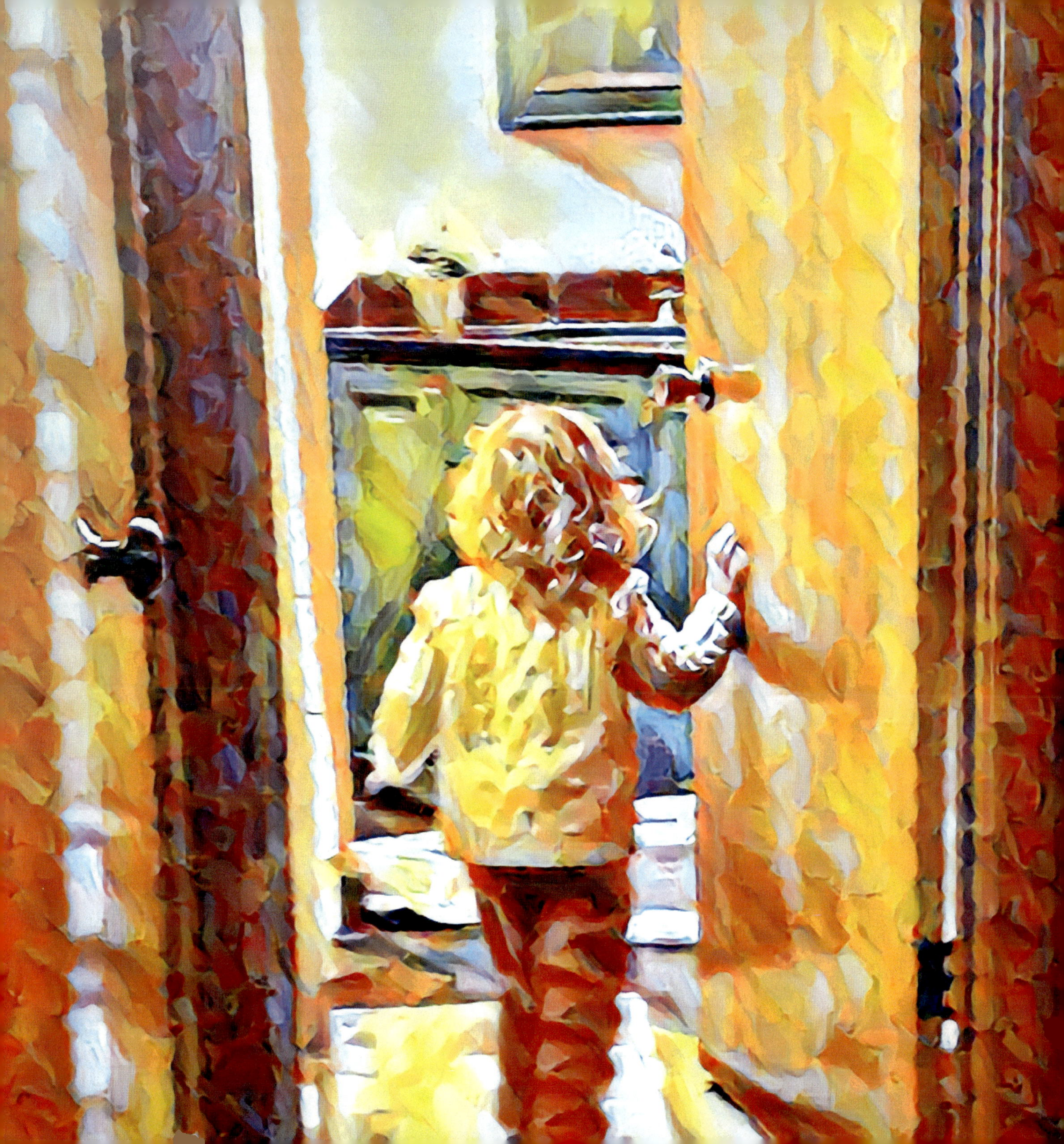

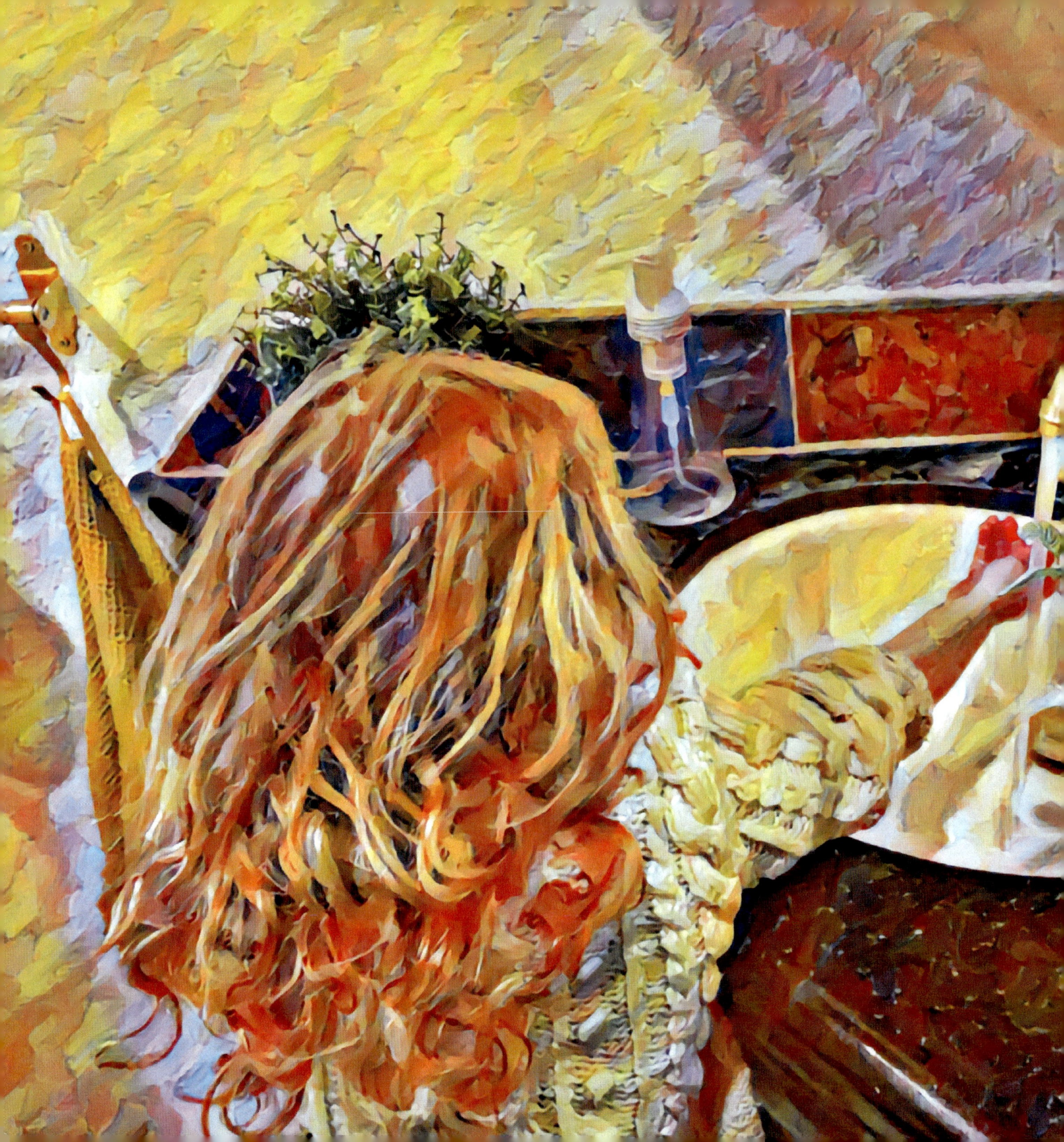

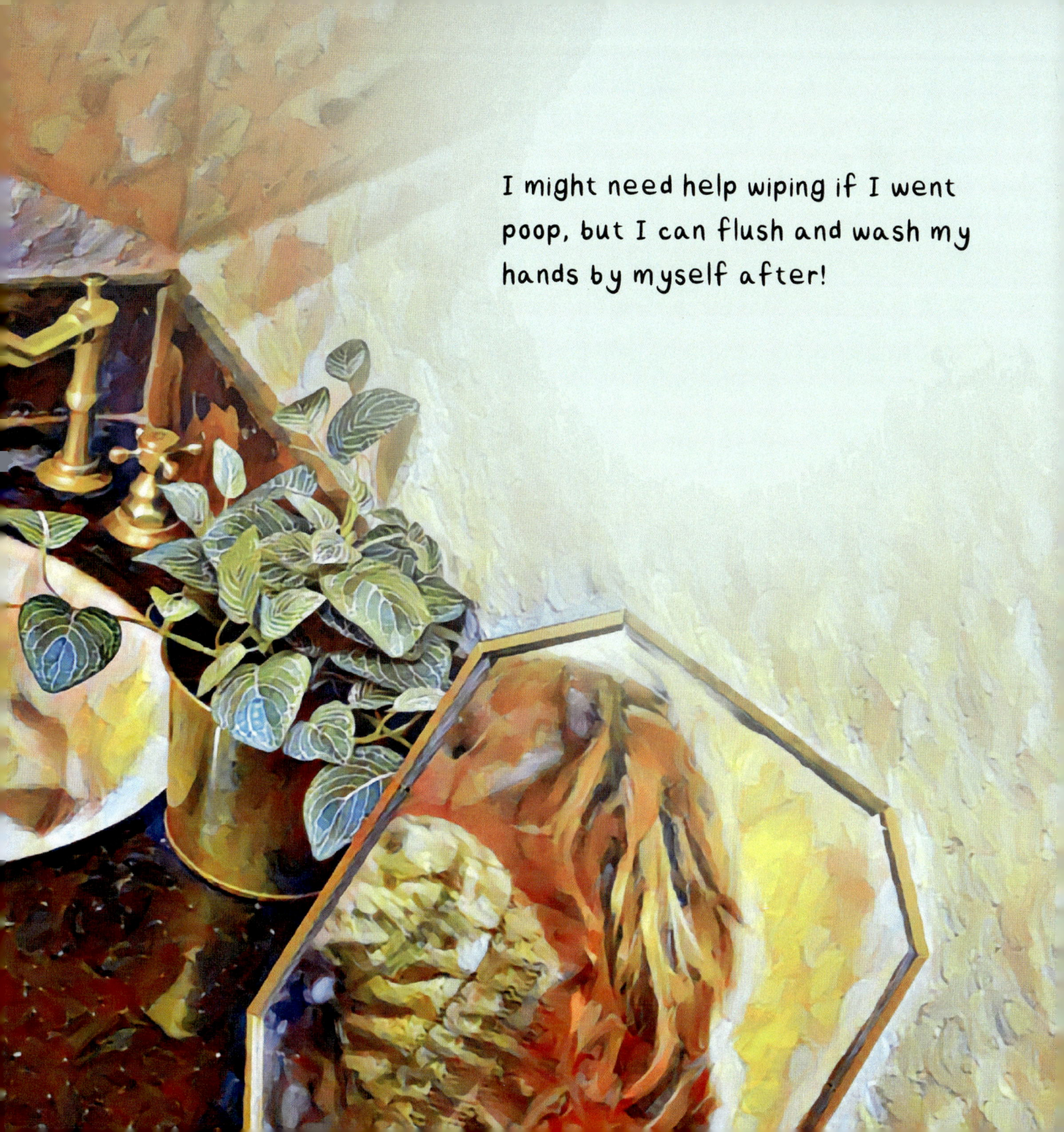

I might need help wiping if I went poop, but I can flush and wash my hands by myself after!

There are special times when I try to go to the bathroom even if I don't feel like it.

I go before long car rides, before bed, and before I go play outside.

Do you have special times when you try even if you don't feel like you have to go?

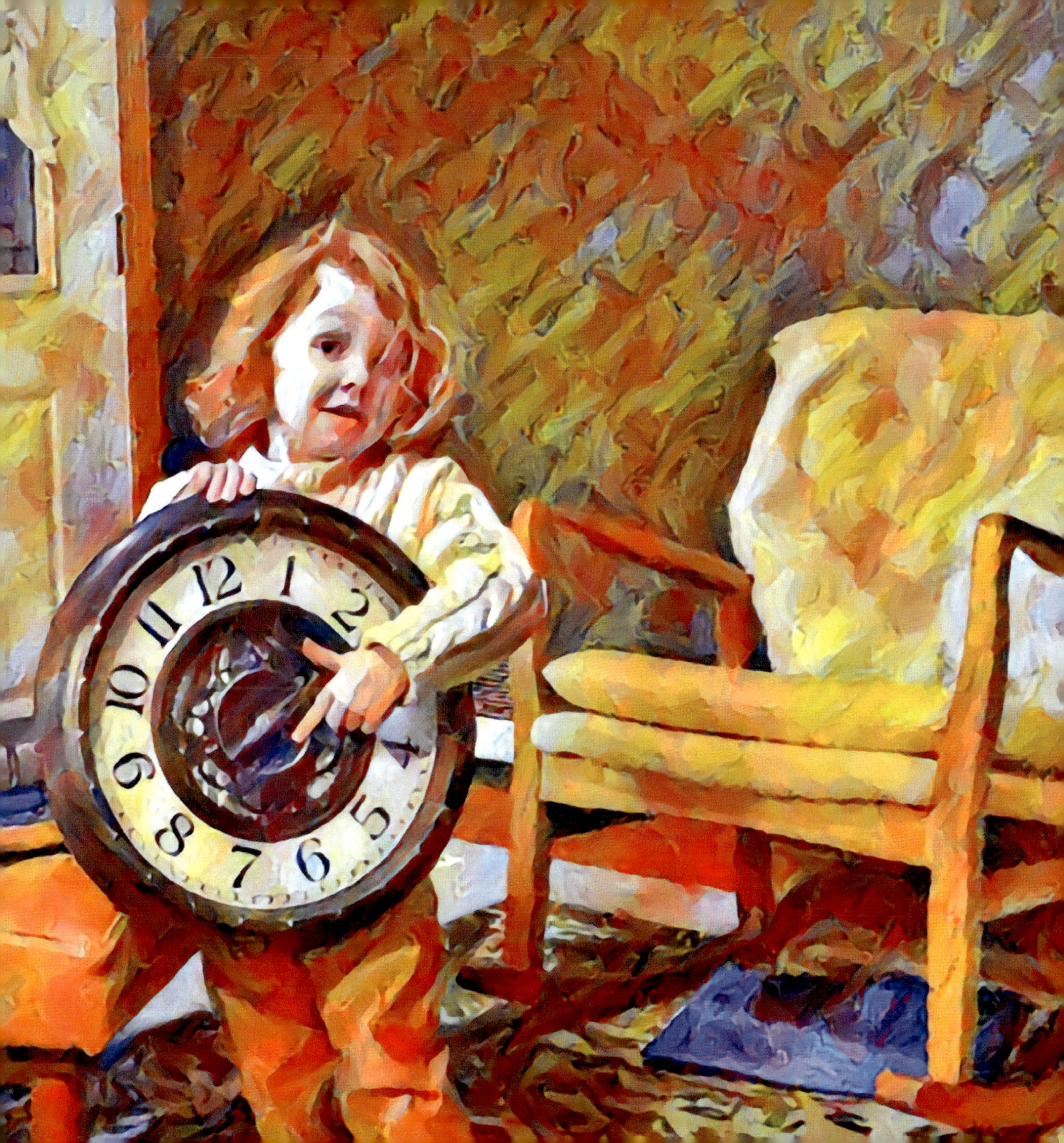

When I listen to my body, I feel good. I am proud to go to the bathroom all by myself.

I am growing up!

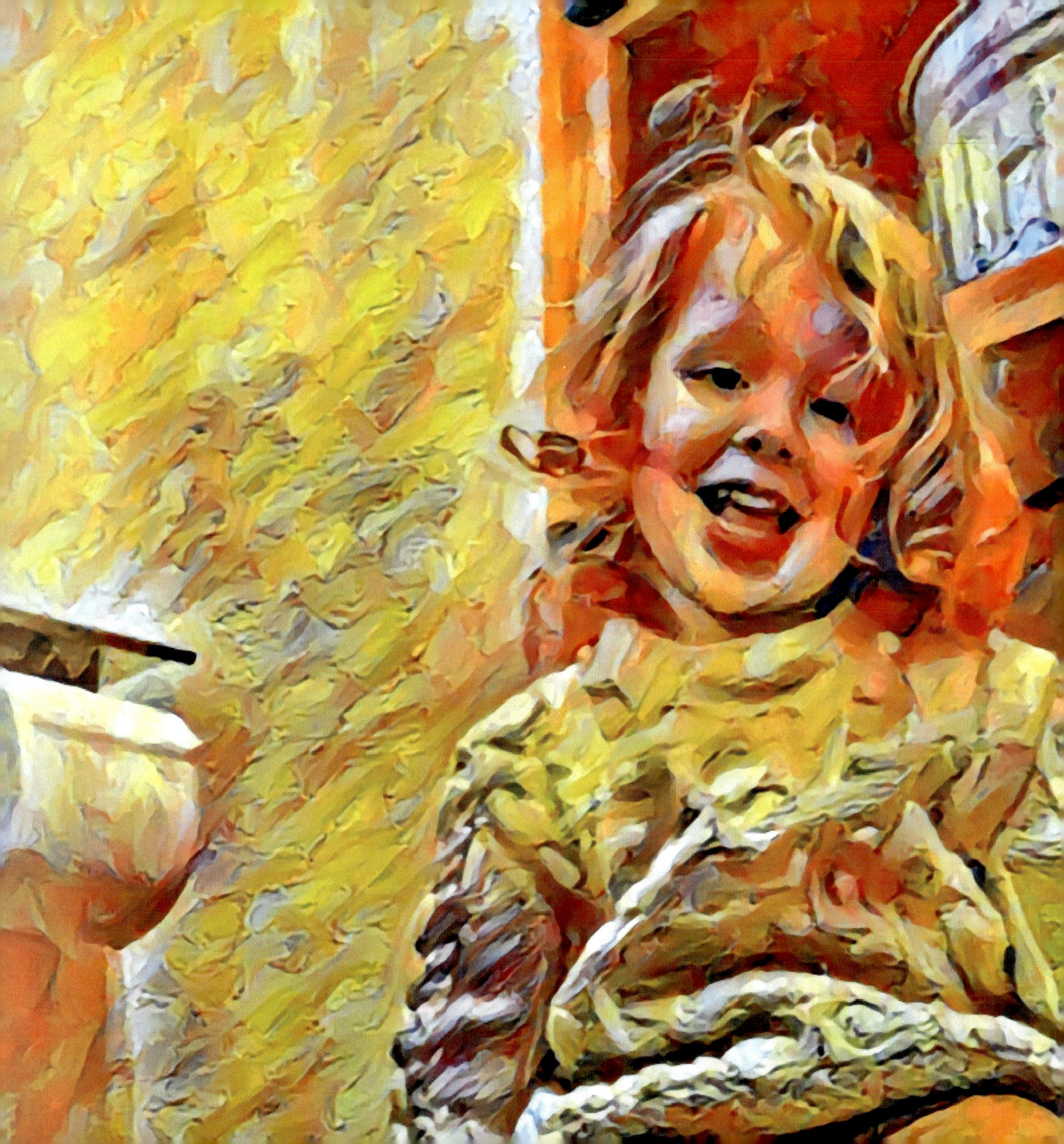

Fin

Made in United States
Orlando, FL
05 May 2024